Easter Island

UNEARTHING ANCIENT WORLDS

Michael Capek

Twenty-First Century Books • Minneapolis

For Chris

The author gratefully acknowledges the contribution of Dr. Georgia Lee and Shawn McLaughlin of the Easter Island Foundation.

Twenty-First Century Books
A division of Lerner Publishing Group, Inc.
241 First Avenue North
Minneapolis, MN 55401 U.S.A.

Website address: www.lernerbooks.com

Library of Congress Cataloging-in-Publication Data

Capek, Michael.
    Easter Island / by Michael Capek.
        p.   cm. — (Unearthing ancient worlds)
    Includes bibliographical references and index.
    ISBN 978–0–8225–7583–2 (lib. bdg : alk. paper)
    1. Easter Island—History. 2. Easter Island—Antiquities. I. Title.
F3169.C26 2009
996.1'8—dc22   2007046454

Manufactured in the United States of America
1 2 3 4 5 6 – PA – 14 13 12 11 10 09

TABLE OF CONTENTS

This statue is one of many that Dutch explorers found when they discovered Easter

INTRODUCTION

In April 1722, three ships sailed through waters more than 2,000 miles (3,219 kilometers) west of Chile, South America. Their captain was Jacob Roggeveen, who worked for the Dutch West India Company. Dutch merchants had formed this company in 1621. Since then the company had explored and traded in South America, Australia, Africa, and many islands in between.

On the morning of April 5—Easter Day—a lookout spotted a tiny island on the horizon. Roggeveen decided to officially claim the island for the Dutch West India Company. In his logbook, he called it Paasch Eyland: Easter Island.

The Dutch explorers rowed ashore. They

In this engraving dated April 10, 1722, Dutch explorers rowing to Easter Island meet locals waiting on the shore. The image was first published in 1728.

hoped to find fresh water and other supplies. But they found only a barren, windswept island. From their ships, they thought they had seen yellow sand coating the island. But it turned out to be dry, sunbaked grass.

A group of people gathered on the beach to meet the sailors. The islanders had tattoos and pierced ears. Some had earlobes that stretched down to their shoulders. These islanders seemed friendly enough at first. But then some of them began to grab hats and clothing from the startled sailors. When one tried to grab a gun from one of the men, the Dutch panicked. They fired into the crowd. They killed ten or twelve of the island's people and wounded many more. The terrified islanders fled. But, remarkably, some of them returned a short time later. They brought the visitors bananas, yams, chickens, and sugarcane. They seemed to have forgotten or forgiven the killings.

The Dutch sailors began to explore the island. They discovered

something both amazing and puzzling. Everywhere they looked, they saw gigantic statues. Some of these figures perched on platforms. These platforms rose 5 to 10 feet (1.5 to 3 meters) high. Other statues stood half buried in the earth. Some were 30 or 40 feet (9 or 12 m) tall.

In his log, Roggeveen included a description of these stone figures. He never got very close to the statues. But from what he saw and heard, Roggeveen thought that carved patterns decorated their surfaces.

This drawing from 1777 shows an Easter Islander wearing a headdress and with elongated earlobes.

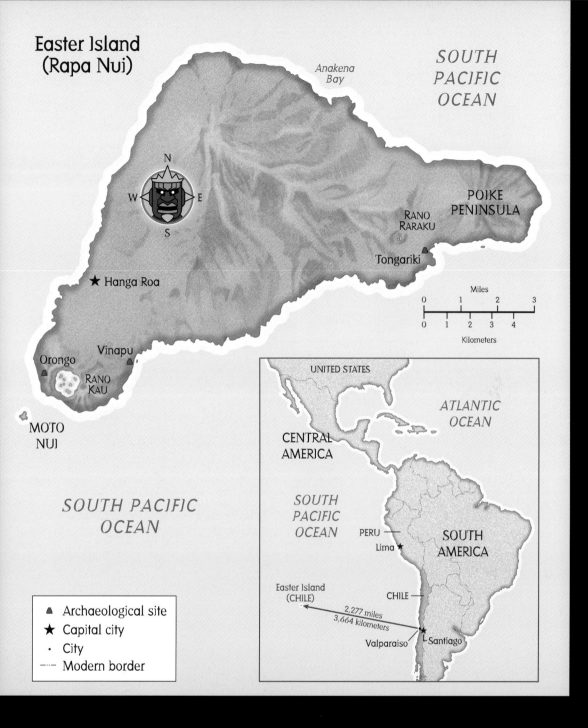

Easter Island (Rapa Nui)

Anakena Bay

SOUTH PACIFIC OCEAN

N
W — E
S

POIKE PENINSULA

RANO RARAKU

Tongariki

★ Hanga Roa

Miles
0   1   2   3
0   1   2   3   4
Kilometers

Vinapu
Orongo
RANO KAU

MOTO NUI

SOUTH PACIFIC OCEAN

UNITED STATES

ATLANTIC OCEAN

CENTRAL AMERICA

SOUTH PACIFIC OCEAN

PERU
Lima ★

SOUTH AMERICA

Easter Island (CHILE)

CHILE

2,277 miles
3,664 kilometers

Valparaiso   Santiago

▲ Archaeological site
★ Capital city
• City
--- Modern border

Huge hats or crowns perched high on some statues' heads. Because of their shape, some Dutch sailors called these headpieces "baskets." Roggeveen guessed that the statues probably represented island gods or important leaders from the past.

The visitors were most puzzled by one question. How had the islanders moved these giant statues into place? The island's people appeared to

—Jacob Roggeveen, 1722

These *moai* statues wear the "baskets," or headpieces, that Roggeveen and his crew found fascinating.

have few materials or tools, such as rope or wood. "At first, these stone figures caused us to be filled with wonder," Roggeveen later wrote. "We could not understand how it was possible that people who [do not have] heavy or thick timber, and also stout [rope] . . . had been able to erect them."

The explorers kept talking about this question. They also took a closer look at the statues. They decided that maybe the statues were not solid stone as they seemed to be. In his logbook, Roggeveen wrote that his crew had made "the discovery, on removing a piece of the stone, that [the statues] were formed out of clay or some kind of rich earth." He added that it looked as though many small, thin pieces of stone coated the figures.

A week later, Roggeveen and his men sailed away. They had found little of value to them on Easter Island. And the islanders had nothing much to trade. The Dutch left little mark on the island, aside from its name.

Fifty years later, Spanish explorers arrived at Easter Island. Don Felipe Gonzalez de Haedo led this 1770 expedition. Like the Dutch, the Spanish sailors were awestruck by the giant statues. Islanders told Gonzalez that they called these statues *moai*.

Gonzalez soon saw that the statues really were made of solid stone. They were not molded clay, as the Dutch had thought. The hand-carved moai weighed many tons each. But like Roggeveen, Gonzalez did not believe that the islanders he met could put up such grand monuments.

After six days, the Spanish left Easter Island. They were searching for lands rich in silver and gold, not stone.

EASTER ISLAND FAST FACTS

- Easter Island lies more than 2,200 miles (3,541 km) west of Chile. It is 2,515 miles (4,048 km) east of Tahiti (an island in the South Pacific Ocean). The island is roughly triangular in shape and about 65 square miles (168 sq. km) in area. Easter Island is one of the most isolated inhabited places on Earth.

- The name "Easter Island" came from the Dutch sailors who visited it in 1722. But modern islanders prefer the name Rapa Nui. The island's language and the islanders themselves are often called Rapanui.

- Experts think that people have lived on Easter Island since about A.D. 400. They believe that these people are of Polynesian descent. Over the years, the island's population has ranged from as high as several thousand to as low as 110. Its modern population is estimated to be 3,500 to 4,000. Most people live in the main town, Hanga Roa.

- The island's most famous feature is the giant stone heads called moai. Experts don't agree on exactly when islanders created the moai. But the statues probably date back to between A.D. 1000 and 1600. So far, people have found 887 moai. Many more may still be buried or hidden. The largest moai is almost 72 feet (22 m) tall and weighs about 155 tons (141 metric tons). The smallest standing moai is only 3.8 feet (1.1 m) tall.

- Easter Island's people have suffered many misfortunes over the years. Experts still are not exactly sure why they stopped carving moai. But modern Easter Islanders remain proud of their heritage and of the amazing stone faces that stare across the landscape.

James Cook was a British explorer who sailed to Easter Island in 1774. Cook was the first to map Newfoundland and made the first European contact with the eastern coastline of Australia and the Hawaiian Islands.

In 1774 British explorer James Cook sailed the ship *Resolution* to Easter Island. Cook and his crew were fascinated and bewildered by the great stone statues. Unlike earlier explorers, Cook and his men took more time to investigate. They saw that many of the statues were on their sides. They had apparently fallen or had been pushed over since Gonzalez's visit. Cook was too ill to go ashore with his men. But he wrote in his journal about what his crew saw. "On the east side near the sea," he wrote, "they met with three platforms of stone-work, or rather the ruins of them. On each had stood four of those large statues, but they were all fallen down from two of them, and also one from the third." Cook added, "All except one were broken by the fall, or in some measure defaced."

Like the Dutch, the British sailors first thought that the statues were clay, not stone. They guessed that islanders had mixed and molded clay on the spot and let it bake in the sun. But when they examined the statues up close, they quickly learned otherwise. When they struck a statue with an iron object, the stone did not easily break or chip. It was definitely stone. And it was solid—not a hollow shell. But like earlier visitors, they wondered how this was possible. The island's people had little food to eat. They were thin, and many wore tattered clothing. The island offered few resources. How could these islanders ever create and erect such huge stone statues?

In spite of the magnificent moai, Cook's final opinion of Easter Island was not very good. He wrote, "No nation need contend for the honour of the discovery of this island," he wrote. "There can be few places which afford less convenience for shipping than it does. Here is no safe anchorage; no wood for fuel; nor any fresh water worth taking on board. Nature has been exceedingly sparing in her favors to this spot." He went on, "Nothing but necessity will induce anyone to touch at this isle, unless it can be done without going much out of the way."

The explorers returned to Europe. But word about Easter Island had started to spread among sailors and businesspeople. Everyone thought the place was interesting and mysterious. But it contained no natural resources for whaling or exploration ships. Many of these ships passed by the island during the 1700s. But few paused for more than a day or two, if they stopped at all. Little record remains of the island or its people during this period.

A TERRIBLE FATE

It was not until the 1800s that people decided Easter Island had something of value, after all. Beginning around 1820, American whaling ships and others began kidnapping Easter Islanders to sell as slaves. In 1862 slave ships from Chile and other South American countries came to the island. The crews of these ships carried away thousands of islanders, forcing them into servitude and misery. By 1877 the population of Easter Island had dropped to only 110 people. Most of the islanders left were too old, young, sick, or weak to work.

This painting by American artist William Bradford, created in 1859, shows whaling ships at sea. It hangs in the Smithsonian American Art Museum in Washington, D.C.

The sudden removal of thousands of people ripped a hole in the island's culture. Chiefs, elders, and artists were some of the people who became slaves. With them went centuries of stored knowledge. They may well have held the answers to questions that have mystified the world ever since.

Throughout the 1800s, European ships continued to stop at the island occasionally. Instead of natural resources or slaves, they wanted the island's artworks. In addition to the moai, Easter Island held many smaller pieces of art. These beautiful stone and wooden carvings were hundreds

A Stolen Friend

In 1868 the British warship HMS *Topaze* arrived at Easter Island. Its crew planned to collect artifacts. The crew also decided to bring a moai back to Great Britain. Most statues were far too heavy to move. But the sailors found one smaller, 4-ton (3.6-metric ton) figure. It stood half buried in an ancient ceremonial center known as Orongo. The beautiful statue had many interesting and puzzling symbols carved on its back. It also had a coating of red and white paint.

A group of about two hundred people helped move the statue to the *Topaze* by raft. During the loading, the bright paint (an important archaeological clue) washed off. The islanders seemed sad to see the statue go. They told the ship's crew that the statue's name was Hoa Hakananai'a. The name means "stolen or lost friend." But Hoa Hakananai'a never went home. It still stands in London's British Museum.

Easter Islanders helped the crew of the *Topaze* move Hoa Hakananai'a *(left)* down to the shore. The statue was then taken by raft to the ship.

Mystery Messages

Early Easter Islanders wrote in a script called rongo-rongo. This writing is made up of picturelike symbols. Visitors find it carved on wooden tablets. Many experts think these symbols are a key to unraveling Easter Island's mysterious past. But so far, no one has been able to translate the rongo-rongo tablets.

This stone found on Easter Island is inscribed with writing called rongo-rongo.

of years old. Collectors prized them.
Europeans bought or stole these pieces of the island's history. They took them to museums far away. People in Germany, Great Britain, and beyond marveled at Easter Island's ancient art. Fortunately, most moai were far too large and heavy to carry. But many other important artifacts and relics were not.

As the end of the 1800s approached, most people still did not know much about Easter Island. Those islanders who remembered anything about the place's history and culture were slowly fading away. Only a few old people still survived. Their grandfathers and grandmothers had told them secret tales and tidbits about the past. They knew stories of the island's beginnings and the names of chiefs. Some of them could read carved writings called *rongo-rongo*. They remembered the ancient songs and rituals, the true meaning of the moai, and the ceremonies surrounding them. But as these elders died, all this information was in danger of being lost forever.

The shore of Easter Island is rocky. It is one of the most isolated inhabited places on Earth.

CHAPTER one

THE LAND OF STONE GIANTS

The USS *Mohican* appears off the coast of Easter Island on December 18, 1886. The ship is part of the U.S. Navy. When it arrives, a few islanders swim and paddle out to the ship to meet the visitors. The meeting is tense. Most visitors to the island in the past have come with bad intent. It takes a while for the islanders to trust these sailors. But the Americans explain they have only come to explore the island. They want to pay islanders to be their guides. They also want to talk to local people. They promise to listen to their ideas and memories.

The islanders finally invite a party of eleven investigators ashore. Their leader is William Judah Thomson. He is the ship's paymaster—the officer in charge of paying the crew. Thomson is also the only member of the *Mohican* crew with much experience studying such historical treasures.

Thomson and his team plan to collect samples of plant and animal life. They also want to gather some historical artifacts. The visitors are especially interested in the island's statues. They also want to study platforms called *ahu*. They think the ahu are burial sites and that many statues once sat on top of them. Previous visitors have described these

amazing sights. But no one has ever made a detailed list of the island's statues and other relics.

Thomson immediately goes to look at some of the famous statues. Hardly any of them are still standing. Only a few half-buried moai are upright on the slopes of Rano Raraku, an extinct volcano on the island's southeastern tip. Many of the fallen giants are broken.

It's easy to see how previous visitors might have thought the statues were made of clay. They are massive. But the *Mohican* investigators look carefully at the huge broken pieces lying in the grass. They can clearly see that people carved each moai from a huge piece of stone. But what or who do the statues represent?

Even in their damaged state, the statues fill the investigators with wonder. The faces are long, with deep hollows under their heavy brows. Their noses are long and flared at the nostrils. The upper lips are short, and the mouths appear to be puckered or sneering. If they were standing upright, their gazes would be pointed slightly upward, as if they were studying the sky. Their expressions are all different. Some look serious, and some slightly amused. Others appear snobbish, thoughtful, disgusted, or downright angry. No wonder islanders sometimes call the statues *aringa ora,* or living faces.

CROWNS OF STONE

The morning after they arrive, the explorers set out to see the island. A few local guides lead the way. Soon the group passes a quarry (a place where workers extract stone or rock). The quarry held a soft volcanic stone called red tufa. Ancient islanders once got stone here for making crownlike headdresses called *pukao.* These crowns sit on some statues' heads.

Wedges of basalt and obsidian (types of hard volcanic rock) lie scattered about the quarry. These wedges are tools called *toki.* Long ago, workers left them here. One of the American investigators picks up a toki. He chips away at the soft tufa. Cutting it takes little effort.

Left: This toki is made of basalt. Easter Island workers used these wedge tools to shape the pukao (headdresses) out of volcanic tufa *(below).*

One of the guides explains that workers placed pukao on only the most respected moai. These were images of great chiefs or mighty warriors. Perhaps they were supposed to represent headdresses that important people once wore. He points out several huge round pukao lying half buried in the red, powdery soil. They look like discarded wheels from some gigantic carriage. The largest crown here is 13 feet (3.9 m) across. It weighs nearly 5 tons (4.5 metric tons). Those found in other parts of the island weigh between 3 and 20 tons (2.7 and 18 metric tons).

The lava rock is easy to carve. Still, the visitors can see that it would have taken a long time to make even one of the huge pukao. Thomson guesses that it must have taken a month or two, depending on how many people worked on it.

Everyone is wondering the same thing. How did islanders ever get these heavy stones onto the statues' heads?

The guides answer that it was *mana*. Another islander explains that mana is a kind of power or magic. Certain chiefs and wise men and women

A Rapanui Legend

Long ago, an old woman lived near the mountain where the statues were made. This woman possessed great mana. Whenever the carvers finished a statue, the old woman used these magic powers to move the statues to ahu all over the island. She simply spoke, and a great stone flew to its new position. All she asked in return for these feats was that the workers share their food with her.

One day, the workers caught a lobster. They cooked and ate it, leaving nothing for the old woman. When she found out, the old woman was furious. She lifted her arms. "Fall down!" she cried in a loud voice. Immediately, statues all over the island toppled over. Some fell on their faces. Others landed on their backs. Many broke as they tumbled. Not one was left standing. The stone carvers dropped their tools and ran away. They never went back to the quarry again.

once used it for good or evil. The guides say that mana is how the statues walked across the island to their platforms and stood upright.

Later, Thomson and his team talk about another possible explanation. Perhaps many people worked together to roll the heavy pukao up a ramp. Islanders could have made this ramp out of packed earth and stones. Thomson suggests that such a ramp might have risen to the height of a statue's head. Once the crown was in place, workers could have removed the ramp. This method would have taken quite a bit of time and effort. But compared to carving and moving moai, placing pukao must have been fairly easy, Thomson says.

"I was told by an old man that the statues are supposed to represent actual people of the past and are monuments to their memory. The stone images were never worshiped . . . but stood as reminders of great and distinguished ancestors. . . . The carvers of the stone statues were most highly esteemed and honored. The skills and knowledge were passed down from father to son, through many generations. Some present Easter Islanders still proudly proclaim their descent from some long-ago image-makers, and speak of their ancestors with intense pride, as one might who is a descendent of George Washington or one of our founding fathers."

—William Judah Thomson, 1891

Next, the guides take the investigators to Rano Kau. This extinct volcano rises on the island's southwestern tip. On the mountain's southwestern side, overlooking the ocean, is the ancient village of Orongo.

BIRDMEN AND WARRIORS

Nearly fifty low stone buildings perch on this high, windy ridge. Some have fallen or been knocked down over the years. These buildings are low domed structures. They look a bit like stone igloos. They have no windows, and each has only one low, tunnel-like door. These entrances are so narrow that visitors have to crawl on hands and knees or wriggle on their bellies to enter.

This is the place of the bird ceremonies, the island guides say in hushed voices. As darkness falls, the guides suggest that the group take shelter in one of the buildings. The men scoot inside, one by one. It's damp and eerie inside. Cold wind wails through openings in the ancient stones.

The ancient stone houses of Orongo hold carvings of birdmen and other creatures.

The guides begin to tell tales of Orongo's meaning and history. A candle's glow reveals carved and painted images of birds and sea creatures on the ceilings and walls. There are fantastic faces too—strange beasts, half-men and half-birds. The guides call them birdmen. The guides also describe the annual festivals once held here. All the while, Thomson tries with cold, trembling hands to scribble down what they say. The team's artist struggles to draw copies of the images. The ancient carvings and paintings almost seem alive, wriggling in the flickering candlelight.

The Birdman Cult

Long ago, Easter Islanders gathered at Orongo each spring. They came for the birdman cult ceremonies. Priests and islanders stayed in Orongo's stone shelters during the festival. The event centered on local seabirds. These birds and their eggs provided valuable food for the islanders, who viewed the birds as sacred. Thousands of the birds nested on a tiny island called Motu Nui. Moto Nui lies about 2 miles (3 km) off Easter Island's rugged southwestern shore.

During the ceremonies, young men of the island competed in a race. First, they had to climb down a steep 1,000-foot (305 m) cliff to the sea. Then they swam to Motu Nui. Once there, they struggled up steep rocks to find the first egg of the year. The person who returned the unbroken egg to Orongo was the winner. This man's chief then became the birdman for the coming year. Islanders believed that the birdman was a human form of Make-Make, the creator of the universe.

Petroglyphs (rock carvings) of dancing birdmen decorate this boulder at Orongo.

On December 23, the team makes its way along the north coast to Anakena Bay. Legends say that Hotu Matu'a, the mythical father of Easter Island, landed with his followers here. Perhaps Hotu Matu'a was a real king. Maybe legends about his deeds grew out of things several different warrior-kings did. It all happened so long ago that no one is sure anymore.

The team arrives on the flat plain behind Anakena's beach. Small platforms, ahu tombs, and ruined dwellings from ages past cover the area. Nearby is Paro, a fallen stone giant at least 30 feet (9 m) long. It appears to be in the best state of preservation of any found near ahu around the island. The guides say that Paro represented some unknown female chief or wise woman. They also say it was the last image completed and put in place before statue making stopped altogether.

Paro was pushed over only about twenty-four years ago, one guide says. Before that time, it spent many years as the island's only statue still standing on a platform.

But who destroyed the statues, and why? Thomson and his team hope to answer these important questions. But the guides are not sure. All they know are old stories they have heard. They tell tales of great wars that once raged on the island. These battles ruined the moai and ahu, they say. But exactly when and why these wars took place, they do not know.

A King's Arrival

According to legend, there was once a mighty king named Hotu Matu'a. He lived with his people on Hiva, an island paradise. They had freshwater and plenty of yams, sweet potatoes, and palm nuts to eat. But all was not well. A war chief had taken over part of the island. He declared war on Hotu Matu'a and his people. As the threat of violence rose, Hotu Matu'a decided it would be best to find a new home. The king and more than four hundred of his people boarded two huge boats. Then they sailed into the sunrise to their new home.

The sailors pointed their boats eastward. They steered using the stars, the wind, and the clouds. They also used ocean currents and the movements of fish and birds as guides. After six weeks at sea, they found a small, well-forested island. They were overjoyed to find a new home. They believed that the great spirit Make-Make had given it to them. They vowed to honor him forever.

These moai are half buried in the stone quarry at Rano Raraku. Thomson and his team

CHAPTER two
SLEEPING GIANTS

Beginning on December 25, 1886, William Thomson and his *Mohican* team start exploring the stone quarries at Rano Raraku. They carefully examine a peninsula called Poike one afternoon. This flat plain lies east of Rano Raraku's quarries. Ahu cover the plain. Some of these platforms once held moai. The statues lie scattered about where they fell. Some are half or almost entirely buried in rubble. The team takes apart what is left of several ahu. Workers dig up the foundations below. The stone platforms are very sturdy. Some have bases that go down 6 feet (1.8 m) or more underground. The explorers find human remains in various stages of decay in the ahu.

The team also notices that the dirt beneath the ahu is rich and free of stones. But outside the foundation walls, the thin dirt holds many large stones. This discovery shows that past workers brought the dirt here from somewhere else. They must have carefully smoothed and prepared it before building the platforms.

A sailor stands beside an ahu wall in this photograph from Thomson's 1886 investigation of Easter Island.

Among the ahu ruins are many pieces of stone images and pukao. Thomson studies these clues carefully. He concludes that islanders must have built, destroyed, and repaired the platforms several times over the centuries.

Next, it is time to examine Rano Raraku's crater. The extinct volcano is 525 feet (160 m) high and 2,133 feet (650 m) across. It was where artists crafted Easter Island's stone statues. Long ago, islanders carved workshops out of the crater's walls. These spaces are high on the crater's southern and western sides.

The team counts sixty-three completed statues in the crater. Forty of them are standing, partially buried in dirt and rock debris. The explorers believe that these statues must have been ready for placement elsewhere on the island. But no one can guess how the early islanders would have moved the huge stones out of the crater.

MAGICAL TALES

A little digging inside the crater turns up more of the carvers' stone tools. Many people obviously worked here over a long period of time. None of the party can tell when exactly. There are many local stories about the statues and their creation. But how accurate the stories are is not clear. They seem to be mostly tales of magic, fantastic feats, heroes, and mythical beings. Islanders speak of long-ago days when the statues walked around in the darkness. Sometimes kings and chiefs ordered them to move. Other times they walked on their own. And the stories never say exactly when things occurred.

Some team members believe that the quarry workshops were still working when Cook's group visited in 1774. But Cook did not stay very long. He and his men visited this part of the island only briefly. His journal says nothing about statue carving.

This tool is called a toki. Workers and artists used toki to carve the stone in Rano Raraku's quarries.

The crew spends another day studying workshops on the west side of Rano Raraku. These workshops sit on flat terraces cut into the crater's outer slope. They are like huge steps up the mountain's side. They are even bigger than those on the inside. Workers here used toki like the ones the team saw at the pukao quarry. The tools lie all around.

Unfinished statues still lie in many of these workshops. They look like sleeping giants. Thomson and the others cannot agree on how the carvers moved completed statues down to the plain below. Someone suggests that perhaps they just wrapped ropes around the moai

These unfinished statues lie in a stone quarry on Easter Island.

and slid them down the steep cliff. Loggers use this method with large trees. But the stone statues are much heavier than trees. Besides, moai coming down from upper levels would have slid over statues still being carved. This would have destroyed both the statue being lowered and those under construction. And no one is even sure ancient islanders even had rope.

"The work of lowering the huge images from the upper terraces to the bottom of the crater and [from there] over the wall and down into the plain below, was of great magnitude [effort], and we are lost in wonder that so much could be accomplished. . . . The average weight of these statues would be something between 10 and 12 tons [9 and 11 metric tons], but some are very large and would weigh over 40 tons [36 metric tons]. It is possible that a slide was made, upon which the images were launched to the level ground below; a number of broken and damaged figures lie in a position to suggest that idea, but from the bottom of the crater they were transported up and over the wall and thence over hill and dale to various points all over the island."

—William Judah Thomson, 1891

The team counts 150 statues remaining at Rano Raraku quarry. Some stand at the bottom of the mountain. They are finished and were apparently lowered from above. Many others are still nestled in their workshop hollows. Some are amazingly huge. The largest moai found on the island lies unfinished in one of the central quarry workshops. It is 70 feet (21 m) long and 15 feet (4.6 m) across. Its head alone is 29 feet (8.8 m) long.

THE STONES OF VINAPU

With the help of the Rapanui guides, the *Mohican* team counts 555 statues on the island. Thomson thinks that many more are still buried or hidden. Most of the statues the group has counted lie broken near old stone platforms along the coast. Others are scattered over the plains farther inland. It seems as though ancient islanders were moving these statues toward some destination when they suddenly abandoned them.

The group also stops at Vinapu. Vinapu was once a large village or ceremonial center. It lies near the sea on Rano Kau's slopes, across the crater from Orongo. Huge stones here form the wall of a platform facing the sea. Thomson clears away dirt and debris from stones. He is amazed at what he sees. Many of the perfectly placed blocks weigh 5 tons (4.5 metric tons) or more. And they fit almost perfectly against one another. But Thomson is not sure how ancient stoneworkers were able to

Right: A close-up view of the stone wall at Vinapu shows how perfectly the pieces fit together in the structure *(below)*.

shape and fit the stones so precisely with their basic tools. He imagines workers scrubbing and grinding away at the stones. Perhaps they rubbed a mixture of water and sand across the stone surface over and over again until it was smooth and flat.

Thomson also notices overlapping joints cut deep into the stone. Workers must have used stone tools to make these joints. Perhaps many of them chipped away at the blocks of stone for days, weeks, or even months. Thomson feels that this platform and wall are some of the most amazing structures of ancient times.

Several local people tell Thomson that Vinapu's ahu was the last one that workers built on the island. They believe it was supposed to hold the 70-foot-long (21 m) statue the team saw in the quarry. The stories say that before workers could finish and move the giant moai, civil war erupted among different tribes on the island.

Thomson records the Rapanui words he hears the islanders use as they tell of those terrible days. With their help, he pieces together a story of warring groups. The tales tell of death on a massive scale. Terror and devastation spread across the small island.

Thomson realizes that these stories might not be completely accurate. Memories and tales may have grown and changed over the years. But they still form a

"Many years after the death of the Great Parent, Hotu Matu'a, the island was equally divided between his descendants, the 'short ears,' and a 'long-eared race.' A great feud developed between these two different peoples. Eventually, a series of bloody wars were fought. . . . Image-builders and platform-makers were drawn into the conflict . . . and, in a spirit of revenge, platforms were destroyed and images thrown down whenever opportunity offered."

—William Judah Thomson, 1891

connection to the past. They offer a reason for the ruin the investigators see all around them. And Thomson continues gathering memories and tales from the islanders.

After eleven days on the island, it is time for the *Mohican* crew to leave. The report that Thomson takes back to the United States is somewhat sad. Easter Island's history appears to have been violent. At some point, the island's population apparently grew too large. There wasn't enough food. Trees to build houses and to burn as fuel disappeared. Fighting for resources led to full-fledged war. Thomson has even heard horrible tales of cannibalism (humans eating other humans). And after the war ended, still more misery lay ahead. Slave ships carried away many children and grandchildren of the war's survivors.

William Thomson gives one last look at the ruined glory of former ages. Given its painful past, it is small wonder that the island looks as it does as he sails away.

Many moai have carvings on their backs. When Katherine Routledge came to Easter Island to explore in the early 1900s, she took an interest in these carvings.

CHAPTER three
THE MANA EXPEDITION

The *Mana* looks small and helpless as it bobs on the blue waves off Easter Island's shore. The yacht belongs to a British couple named Scoresby and Katherine Routledge. They arrived here on March 12, 1914. Since then the Routledges have been studying the island's culture and archaeology.

Some of their boat's crew and a few local people also help them. They have already begun thoroughly exploring the island. They want to find and learn about Rapa Nui's most important ancient relics.

The Routledges are not trained archaeologists. But both spent several years studying ethnic groups and communities in Africa. They have written about early civilizations and studied ancient artifacts. They have also read everything available about Easter Island. And they are eager to add even more to the world's knowledge of this place.

The Routledges arrived at Easter Island aboard their yacht, the *Mana*. It is shown here anchored in Chile's Patagonia Channels on its way to Easter Island in December 1913.

33

Katherine Routledge wanted to study the moai and learn the stories behind them.

"Looked at from the landward side, we may ... [think of] an ahu as a vast theatrical stage, of which the floor runs gradually upwards from the footlights. The back of the stage, which is thus the highest part, is occupied by a great terrace, on which are set up in line the giant images, each one well separated from his neighbor, and all facing the spectator. Irrespective of where he stands, he will ever see them towering above him, clear-cut against the turquoise sky."

—Katherine Routledge, 1919

The Routledges begin carrying out the first true scientific investigation ever done on the island. He focuses on conducting business, collecting artifacts, and exploring caves. She and local assistants will study the ahu and moai. She also hopes to probe the memories of islanders. She wants to discover and apply what they know about their home's past.

DETECTIVE WORK

Katherine Routledge soon begins examining sites around the island. As she does, she refers often to a ragged bunch of handwritten notes in her pocket. These notes are copies of an account that William Judah Thomson wrote twenty-eight years ago. Thomson's detailed report gives her an excellent starting point for her work.

Thomson and his fellow *Mohican* investigators had only had a short stay on the island. But she has more time. She takes many notes about what she sees and finds. She carefully measures moai and ahu. She studies everything closely. She returns to some sites many times. She does not want to miss an important clue.

Thomson wrote in 1886 that islanders had once divided their home into ten or twelve separate sections. Individual family groups called clans lived on and ruled over each section. Katherine Routledge has learned more about this past custom by talking to local people. They tell her that some families still have traditional ties to certain parts of the island. She sets out to write down the details of these ties.

Routledge also focuses on the ahu. She knows that these platforms were once religious sites. Ancient islanders used them for burials. Present-day Rapanui people also use these platforms for burials. But did other religious ceremonies take place at the ahu? She is not sure. But clearly, the past and present continually mix and mingle at the ahu. For example, she finds evidence of ancient and present-day burials side by side inside the large ahu at Tongariki, south of Rano Raraku. And she believes that the stories and memories people have of these places may also be mixtures of fact and fiction. She will try to figure out which is which.

Katherine Routledge took this photograph of a burial place on the coast of Easter Island.

Katherine Routledge has learned that moai once stood on about one hundred of the ahu—about one-third of all the island's burial platforms. Most ahu were originally about 10 to 15 feet (3 to 4.6 m) high and 300 feet (91 m) long. Long ramps led up to some platforms from the side that faced away from the ocean. Flat stones paved the area around and in front of each ramp. These paving stones created huge plazas. They were probably gathering places during ceremonies. The moai themselves stood on narrow, flat terraces near the plaza's edge. The statues faced inland, with their backs to the water. Some ahu held several statues. Others had only one.

She inspects the stones around the edges of some ahu. Many are enormous. Like Thomson, she is amazed at how snuggly they fit together. Not even a knife blade can slip between their joints.

BIRDMEN AND BIRD CHILDREN

Katherine Routledge spends some time exploring Orongo's stone shelters. She crawls into the cramped, windowless buildings. She carries a candle to light her way. She carefully studies and makes drawings of the stone carvings she finds inside. She knows from Thomson's report that the strange beings she sketches are birdmen and other figures connected with those rituals.

Thomson's report also tells her that the main birdman ceremony involved a death-defying race to get the year's first egg of the sooty tern. But she has learned new things while talking to modern islanders. They tell her that

Katherine Routledge made this drawing of Orongo's houses and caves as she studied them.

each year the new birdman danced across the island, carrying the egg. Crowds of people followed in wild celebration, all the way to Rano Raraku. The birdman spent one year living there, in the shadow of the great statue quarries. His fellow islanders treated him as a hero. And when a birdman died, the old stories say, he stayed on this same sacred mountain. Fellow islanders buried birdmen here along with the broken shells of the eggs that made them famous.

Katherine Routledge also hears fascinating tales about another ritual connected with Orongo. It is the ceremony of the *poki-manu,* or bird children. According to the stories, island children used to take part in their own special ceremonies here. First, islanders shaved the children's heads and painted bright white symbols on their bodies. Locals tell her that the children also wore coconuts, hung like heavy necklaces around their necks. This detail shows that palm trees must have grown on Easter Island in the past. She also learns that long ago, most islanders raised chickens for food. The bird children's ceremony involved chicken eggs, instead of seabird eggs.

The children gathered on the same hills where the springtime birdmen contests took place. They danced, sang, and chanted outside one of Orongo's shelters. A sacred moai stood inside this shelter. Carved symbols covered the statue—the same symbols that were painted on the children. The stories call the statue Hoa Hakananai'a. But the crew of the British ship *Topaze* removed this small moai in 1868. Katherine Routledge wonders if that statue's departure marked the end of the bird cult on Easter Island. Historical records and local memories agree that festivals and ceremonies did not continue at Orongo very long afterward.

This rock from Easter Island is carved with a birdman figure holding an egg. This is one of the artifacts collected by Katherine Routledge and is at the British Museum in London.

The important thing is that the birdman ceremonies, the poki-manu rites, and Hoa Hakananai'a all seem connected. Were Orongo and Rano Raraku equally sacred sites to the ancient Rapanui? Katherine Routledge thinks the answer must lie in the quarries at Rano Raraku.

"At the southwest corner [of Rano Raraku stand] the foundations of a house. Here the bird-man remained for a year. . . . As the bird-man gazed lazily forth from the shade of his house, above him were the quarries, with their unfinished work, below him were the bones of his dead predecessors, while on every hand giant images stood for ever in stolid calm. It is difficult to escape from the question: Were the statues on the mountain those of bird-men?"

—Katherine Routledge, 1919

THE ART OF STONE CARVING

Standing on the old volcano's slopes, Katherine Routledge can still see the process ancient stone carvers used. Dozens of moai rest here, in all stages of development and in all positions. She begins to record everything she can about these statues.

First, she studies each one carefully. Her island assistants point out some details. And the longer she looks, the more she can see for herself. She spends many hours in the quarries, recording and thinking about what she notices. Eventually, she is able to recognize which tools workers used to carve each statue. She can even tell exactly where the carvers stood as they worked. To finish some statues, workers had to cut paths deep into the stone face of the quarry. They stood here while they chiseled out the statue's final shape. Katherine Routledge measures these work areas. She even asks islanders to stand in them. Doing so helps her guess how many people probably worked on any given statue and for how long.

Meanwhile, Scoresby Routledge tackles a related question. He wants to figure out exactly how long it would have taken a master carver and helpers to quarry and carve one moai. He thinks and calculates. He uses some of his wife's measurements and findings. He asks local people who know how to cut stone to show him how. Finally, he concludes that a large group of men—perhaps more than fifty—could carve a 30-foot-high (9 m) image in about fifteen days.

BURIED MOAI

Katherine Routledge soon moves on to a different project. She directs workers who excavate (dig out) twenty finished statues on Rano Raraku's outer slope. The team also works to reveal twelve more moai inside the crater. She wants to find out why they are here. She also wants to see what they look like from top to bottom. Nearly all the statues are covered with a thick layer of dirt and dust. Most are at least partly buried in shallow holes. It seems

In this photograph by Katherine Routledge, her husband Scoresby Routledge and other men excavate a statue from the slope of Rano Raraku quarry.

that past islanders dug these holes for this specific purpose. In fact, some of the half-buried moai sit on prepared stone floors deep underground.

These findings show that the hillside moai are not mistakes or castoffs, as some other visitors thought. These moai are finely crafted and finished works of art. Katherine Routledge also notices that ancient workers polished these statues. She thinks they used a rough, sandpaper-like stone called pumice to rub the stone smooth. Pieces of pumice lie scattered around many of the half-buried statues.

And Katherine Routledge soon makes another discovery. Strong winds and blowing rain whip Easter Island almost constantly. Dirt, grit, and salt spray from the ocean wear away stone quickly. These conditions explain the rough and pocked surfaces of the statues that she studies. But she notices that stone that has long been underground looks different. This stone glows with the same hand-polished sheen that it had when it was first carved. Closer inspection reveals hints of this same polished smoothness inside some eye sockets and under some chins. The elements have not dulled these protected spots. Perhaps, she realizes, the moai are not as old as past investigators thought. They may date back only a few hundred years, rather than several thousand.

RING AND GIRDLE

One day, she is digging around two statues inside Rano Raraku's crater. The statues are buried up to their chins. But once she has uncovered them, she sees carvings on their surfaces. The carved design looks like sashes or belts underneath circles. She calls the pattern a "ring and girdle." And she realizes suddenly that she has seen this pattern before on several ahu.

She is even more interested in newer-looking carvings on the back of one statue. Some elderly islanders look at these carvings. They tell her that the designs resemble tattoos and body paintings that the poki-manu wore during ceremonies at Orongo. This news excites her. It means that she has found one of the things she was looking for—a real connection between the birdmen at Orongo and the statue carving at Rano Raraku.

In this photograph taken by Katherine Routledge, a man sits next to a moai that has been excavated from the quarry at Rano Raraku. The ring and girdle pattern is visible on the very bottom of the statue.

Island people continue to tell Katherine Routledge stories and memories. They share different ideas about what the moai might represent. Some stories say the statues may have been gods or folk heroes of earlier people. Others hint that they are portraits of important ancestors. She wonders if some of the moai on Rano Raraku might be images of birdmen. But her collection of traditions shows one thing for certain. A few of the statues were boundary markers. Islanders still use them to mark the borders between family or clan land divisions. She also suspects that some of the great stones were simply ornaments to decorate the barren landscape.

The Routledges' time on Rapa Nui is nearly over. But so many questions remain. Why and how did past islanders raise the stone images? And why did they do all that work only to topple the moai? How did they move 30- and 40-ton (27- and 36-metric-ton) stones across the island? On Rapa Nui, it seems as though even scientific methods and great determination cannot uncover every answer just yet.

This fallen moai was at the Ahu Tongariki on Easter Island. This ahu was restored starting in 1992.

CHAPTER Four

SENOR KON-TIKI

In October 1955, Thor Heyerdahl gazes at an enormous stone figure
lying on the ground. It is the first time he has seen a moai up close. Like
so many before him, he marvels at the size of the old stone face. The
moai, on the other hand, is coolly unaware
of his presence. It faces the sky with the
same expression it has held for centuries.
Meanwhile, yet another group of curious
strangers has come to the island. Like others
before them, they are searching for answers.
They are asking questions that the outside
world has asked for nearly four hundred years.

Forty years have passed since Katherine
and Scoresby Routledge left Easter Island.
Thor Heyerdahl has come here with a team of
experts. They will see what they can make of
Rapa Nui's puzzles.

Heyerdahl is a world-famous Norwegian
adventurer and writer. His adventures have

Thor Heyerdahl, shown here in
1952, arrived on Easter Island in
1955 with a team of experts. They
wanted to try to unlock the secrets
of the island and its history.

earned him the nickname Senor Kon-Tiki. He is not trained in archaeology. But his team includes archaeologists from all over the world. Arne Skjolsvold comes from Norway. William Mulloy works at the University of Wyoming. Carlyle Smith is from the University of Kansas, and Edwin Ferdon works for the Museum of New Mexico. These researchers are eager to discover whatever lies buried beneath the island's thin red soil. They

Senor Kon-Tiki

Thor Heyerdahl's expedition to Easter Island was not his first major journey. The adventure that brought him his fame and his nickname had taken place in 1947. That was when Heyerdahl and a crew set out on a voyage westward from Peru. They sailed a handmade wooden raft called *Kon-Tiki*. Heyerdahl believed that ancient South Americans had sailed such boats into the Pacific centuries before Polynesians arrived from the west. He believed that some of these South Americans had made Easter Island's moai. And he felt certain *Kon-Tiki* would prove his theory.

Kon-Tiki and its crew had a wild 101-day, 4,300-mile (6,920 km) journey. In August 1947, the boat crash-landed in the Tuamotu Islands, near Tahiti. Heyerdahl declared his experiment a success. Many scientists and historians were not convinced. But *Kon-Tiki*'s voyage sparked an interest in Easter Island that led many others to study it. Heyerdahl himself went on to write a book called *Kon-Tiki*. He also made a movie of the same name. It won an Academy Award in 1952. By the time he arrived on the island three years later, Senor Kon-Tiki was a star.

Thor Heyerdahl used this raft made of balsa wood for his expedition in 1947. It is shown here at the Kon-Tiki Museum in Oslo, Norway.

bring modern techniques and tools. They carry maps and drawings made over the years by other visitors. They also have years of field experience. And they have information from Thomson, the Routledges, and others.

Heyerdahl has a deep interest in Easter Island. And he has his own theories about its past. He has paid for this expedition in hopes of finding evidence to support those theories. Many experts—including some of the ones on this trip—do not share his ideas. But Heyerdahl tells his team that it's all right if they disprove his theories. He just wants them to find and learn whatever they can.

A RUINED VILLAGE

In November 1955, William Mulloy and his helpers go to Easter Island's southwestern tip. They begin carefully studying the ruins of Vinapu's village and ahu.

Mulloy first makes a map showing the thousands of stone blocks and other debris in the area. Past investigators noted that the site once included much more than its one massive ahu platform with seven moai. Mulloy's map shows the old ahu's outlines clearly. But Mulloy also notices other rubble and buried stones nearby. They slope inland from the ahu. His trained eyes see that these stones must have once formed a huge ceremonial plaza. Investigating further, he finds that this plaza probably included two more platforms, statues, a village, and other structures. Mulloy also studies a 30-foot (9 m) cliff that drops to the sea behind the ahu. He finds rubble and other clues here. Mulloy concludes that a stone and earthen ramp once sloped up from the sea to the platforms. Perhaps this ramp once connected Vinapu to an ancient harbor below.

To find out more, Mulloy begins excavating the site. He and his team carefully remove earth and debris around the main ahu. They slowly reveal more of the old platform. They marvel at the structure's artistry and workmanship.

Based on weathering and other signs, Mulloy thinks he knows how the ahu's seven moai were once arranged. And he soon makes another discovery. One of the statues he finds shows traces of red and white paint. He thinks the moai once had a striped pattern painted under its chin

William Mulloy studied the stones at Vinapu's village and ahu. He excavated the site to try and figure out the age of the ruins.

and diagonally across its body. Perhaps this design represented tattoos that important chiefs or priests wore in early times. Mulloy thinks that at one time all statues on ahu were brightly painted. What an amazing sight that must have been!

Meanwhile, the excavation continues. Mulloy believes that workers carved and placed the first stones in about A.D. 600 to 700. He bases this date partly on layers he sees in the walls of trenches that the earliest builders dug. The oldest stones lie well below the present ground level. Above them, many levels of soil, dust, and rock have piled up over the centuries. Based on these layers, he believes that workers rebuilt the original platform at least twice over the years. Each time they rebuilt, they tried to use parts of the previous platforms. They also buried the remains of those older structures. Maybe they were trying to hide them.

But why? Mulloy cannot answer that riddle yet.

As his team digs deeper, Mulloy collects pieces of charcoal from the lowest, earliest level of construction. He thinks they are the remains of fires that priests or worshippers once burned among the original stones. He will send these pieces for carbon-dating tests. These scientific tests will give him and other researchers more information about the age of the site.

The slow digging and sifting continues. It looks as if the first stone builders were the most skilled and careful workers. Mulloy thinks that the earliest ahu was an elegant platform. It was shaped like a large altar and probably held no statues. Fine stonework was the builders' main goal.

The next builders worked hundreds of years later. Between about 1200 to 1600, they created a newer and larger platform. They built it around and on top of the earlier ahu. Their stonework was not as careful or precise as that of their ancestors. But these builders were the statue makers. The fantastic statues they carved, moved, and placed here were wonders of art and engineering. To them the ahu platform was only a place to display moai.

The final phase Mulloy finds is the most recent. Islanders probably built and used it between 1680 and 1860. During this time, the first Europeans arrived.

BURYING THE PAST

At some point during this period, violence erupted on the island. People purposely toppled and broke the huge statues here. They pulled nearly all the finely chiseled stones out of their places—even some of the earliest moai. They destroyed the platform. But then, around the same time, they built another ahu. These builders seem to have been rushed. They placed a new platform on top of the previous platforms. They also used stones from the older platforms. And for some reason, they took great trouble to bury all signs of the earlier structures—including the moai. Why did they do this?

"It seems probable that the [ahu] structure was completely conceived and planned before it was begun, with a real feeling for balance and symmetry [balance]. . . . Those who did it were artists as well as craftsmen."

—William Mulloy, 1961

Mulloy has an idea. He thinks that the levels here might show a gradual change in the way past Easter Islanders thought and worshipped. At some point, maybe people here no longer observed or respected the old ceremonies. Perhaps when statue building became the main way to worship, islanders decided to redo the old religious center. And Mulloy thinks that even later, the statue religion fell out of favor. Birdman ceremonies took its place. He firmly believes that these two religions existed together for some time. But eventually one replaced the other. Maybe that shift caused islanders to attack and ruin the statues. Perhaps the people saw the old beliefs as incorrect or even dangerous. They might have wanted to destroy or hide all signs of the earlier faith.

A THREE-MASTED BOAT

While William Mulloy is busy at Vinapu, Edwin Ferdon is high atop Rano Kau. He is at the ruins of Orongo. Ferdon knows that Rano Raraku and Vinapu might hold important

A ceremonial dwelling at Orongo overlooks the ocean. Edwin Ferdon studied these structures.

clues for solving Easter Island's mysteries. But he feels sure that this ancient village is the key to unlocking them. After all, evidence suggests that each statue and ahu may have belonged to only one tribe or clan. Orongo, however, had been a gathering place for everyone on the island. The wise men had met here to read the rongo-rongo. Ferdon concludes that such an important site must have many stories to tell. If Ferdon is right, whatever he finds at Orongo may cast light on everything else the team discovers on the island.

But excavating at Orongo presents unique challenges. The village is perched high on Rano Kau, at the island's narrow southernmost point. It is constantly exposed to the full force of wind and rain. On one side, a sheer cliff drops 1,000 feet (305 m) to the ocean and jagged rocks below. On the other side is the old volcano's steep inner wall. At the bottom of the volcano's crater is a reed-choked lake. Island legend says the lake is bottomless.

Waters and Woods

The lake inside Rano Kau's crater is the largest and deepest on Easter Island. Heyerdahl and others take samples from beneath the lake's surface. Scientists then examine these samples. In the deeper layers, they find many pollen grains from plants that no longer grow on Easter Island. These studies proved that palm trees and other plants once covered the island. These plants would have easily supplied food to support thousands of people. Such forests would also have supplied Easter Islanders with wood and rope to move moai.

The crater inside Rano Kau is visible in this photograph. Rano Kau is located on the southern tip of Easter Island.

First, Ferdon and his helpers dig trenches around some of Orongo's forty stone shelters. In some places, they dig under walls and inside buildings. Some workers find layer upon layer of charcoal as they dig. This burned material makes dark or orange-tinted lines in the trench walls. Lighter-colored levels of windblown dust or debris separate the charcoal layers. The soil also contains the bones of chickens, wild birds, fish, and rats. Easter Islanders ate all of these animals over the years.

Carbon-14 Dating

Archaeologists often use carbon-14 dating to determine the ages of the things they find. All living things contain carbon. And scientists know that one type of carbon atom, C-14, begins to decay at a specific speed the moment a living thing dies. By testing how much C-14 remains in a piece of wood, they can guess its age. Archaeologists can then estimate the ages of objects they find nearby, such as pottery, jewelry, or stone carvings.

DIGGING DOWN

The workers dig slowly downward. They map and label every item they find. Ferdon and his helpers will send many stone tools, charred bits of wood, and other objects to a special lab. Experts at the lab will study them later. Ferdon begins to examine the shelters themselves. He marvels at the way islanders built these dome-shaped structures. He believes that they carefully stacked layer after layer of flat stones on top of one another. Once they had completed a structure's stone walls and roof, builders coated each roof with a layer of thick mud and reeds. This coating kept rain from seeping through. And low, narrow entryways stopped most wind and rain from coming into the sturdy, durable shelters. Such protection is important here. Easter Island's harsh weather can destroy a grass or reed-thatched building in moments.

Ferdon crawls into shelter after shelter. Using a bright flashlight, he examines the walls and ceilings. Old paintings and stone carvings cover many of them. The exact meanings of some of these ancient images and symbols are lost or forgotten. But Ferdon sees many pictures of men with birds' heads. These beings, each carrying a single egg, clearly represent the old birdman cult.

Then Ferdon finds an especially exciting painting in one of the structures. The image shows a boat with a curved front and back. It has three masts and a round sail. Ferdon thinks it looks like a certain type of fishing boat. Peruvians built and sailed such boats centuries ago on South American lakes and on the sea. They made these vessels out of tied bundles of reeds. The result was lightweight boats with great flexibility and strength.

Ferdon quickly sends a worker to find Thor Heyerdahl. He is sure that Senor Kon-Tiki will want to see this boat.

This restored ahu at Tongariki has the largest collection of standing moai on Easter

CHAPTER five

THE MOAI MAKERS

As Edwin Ferdon studies Orongo's images, Arne Skjolsvold excavates statues buried at Rano Raraku's base. These standing statues have puzzled many of Easter Island's visitors. Did finished moai wait here until workers could move them to ahu around the island? Or, as Katherine Routledge wondered, did they sit here to signal that this was a special, sacred place?

Skjolsvold and his workers painstakingly dig around several figures. All are finely finished statues. Past islanders clearly placed them here with care.

Then the diggers make a discovery that connects Rano Raraku to Ferdon's work at Orongo. On the chest of one excavated statue, they find the carved image of a three-masted boat. It looks a lot like the one Ferdon found on the other end of the island. Both of these boat images seem to support Heyerdahl's idea that South Americans landed on Easter Island before Polynesians did. And in the next few days, workers find several more of these pictures on other parts of the island.

CREATING MOAI

A big question still nags the team. How did the statues on Rano Raraku get to the bottom of the volcano? Historians know that workers carved them high above in hillside quarries. Then they somehow lowered the huge moai to this rolling plain. But how?

Earlier explorers found deep holes carved in the solid rock of the volcano rim. Maybe these holes once held thick posts or masts. Many scientists believe that past workers looped ropes around these posts. Then they used the ropes to lower statues safely down the quarry cliff. But islanders may have used some other method to get the statues down. Even after nearly a month of intensive study and investigation, Skjolsvold still cannot say for sure how they moved these moai.

Moai Eyes

In 1978 a student named Sonia Haoa makes an amazing discovery while helping with an excavation at an ahu near Anakena Bay. As she digs, she finds pieces of white coral along with pieces of red scoria (a volcanic stone that islanders used to make pukao). Later, archaeologist Sergio Rapu discovers that these coral fragments fit perfectly into moai eye sockets. These finds prove a longtime theory that ancient people fitted some moai with huge, white eyes. These eyes added greatly to the statue's already impressive appearance. No wonder ancient people may have thought the statues actually came to life when their eyes were in place.

A close-up view of the eye from a moai statue. The coral eye is on display at the Museo Antropológico Padre Sebastián Englert on Easter Island.

Skjolsvold and his team can see how islanders made moai, however. They know that carvers used wedge-shaped picks made of basalt, the island's hardest stone. Workers apparently held the picks in one or both hands. They tapped, pecked, or hammered them against the hard rock.

The team also finds rough pieces of coral scattered around the quarry. Tiny sea creatures make coral. Deep undersea coral reefs lie all around Easter Island. Pieces of the brittle, rocklike material washed up on beaches. In addition to using pumice stone, carvers used these coral pieces to polish finished statues to a smooth sheen.

"The invisible [ancient islanders] . . . seemed to be glorying over us, saying 'Guess how this engineering work was done! Guess how we moved these gigantic figures down the steep walls of the volcano and carried them over the hills to any place on the island we liked!'"

—Thor Heyerdahl, 1958

A NEW IDEA

Skjolsvold can also see evidence of each step the carvers used. He mostly agrees with Katherine Routledge's description of how it was done. But he does have one new idea. It has to do with what the carvers did after they finished the painstaking chipping and chiseling. Skjolsvold thinks that they supported each statue with stacks of small stones while they carefully chipped away the final supporting piece of rock underneath. Then workers used ropes to lower the freed statue to the plain below. There they either hauled it away or placed it in a prepared hole at the foot of the volcano.

Skjolsvold's island assistants also tell him that workers did not carve the statue's eye sockets at the quarry. Legend says that they carved the eyes only after the statue reached its final destination. Ancient people apparently believed that carving a statue's eyes brought it to life and gave it power.

One day, expedition members ask several elder islanders to carve a new moai. These men claim to know how it was done. The archaeologists want to see if past carvers passed down their techniques through many generations. They ask the men to work with the same tools their forefathers used.

The group goes to work. First, they use softer stones to draw an outline on the surface of the quarry stone. Then they begin chipping away at it. After three long days and thousands of blows from the stone picks and chisels, the clear outline of a 20-foot-tall (6 m) statue begins to emerge.

The elderly men are exhausted, however. They stop the work. But Skjolsvold and others conclude that if they had continued, the six men could have finished the statue in twelve to fifteen months. This time frame is much longer than anyone has ever estimated before.

The five-month Heyerdahl study soon ends. No one wants to leave yet, but the expedition's time on Easter Island is over. And after all their work, what team members have actually learned remains a matter of opinion. Heyerdahl feels that they have proven his South American theories. But not everyone agrees. One thing everybody believes firmly, however, is that much work remains. Easter Island has not yet given up all its ancient secrets.

This ancient moai stands at the bottom of Rano Raraku.

THE WORK CONTINUES

After 1960 the study of Easter Island intensifies. The Heyerdahl expedition brought a lot of new attention to the island. One of the strongest calls for continued work comes from expedition member William Mulloy. In 1968 he returns to Easter Island. Over the next eight years, he works there with other experts. They map, excavate, restore, and investigate many sites.

Mulloy's work leads to a major project to survey and describe all the island's moai and important historical sites. Mulloy leads a team of scientists. First, they define thirty-five different sections of Easter Island. Then researchers and archaeologists from the United States and Chile begin mapping and describing all the moai and other important art. They finish all the pieces in each section before moving on to the next. Some of their methods are simple. Workers measure statues with tape measures, take pictures, and make precise sketches. But they also use advanced technology. They use a photography tool that makes exact three-dimensional diagrams of objects. Another method uses information from satellites in space to make extremely precise maps.

This work continues for many years. The U.S.-Chilean effort becomes the Easter Island Statue Project (EISP). By 1982 the EISP has completely surveyed fifteen of the island's thirty-five sections.

William Mulloy returned to Easter Island to do more research in the 1960s. He is shown here near Orongo in 1973.

Another project begins in 1992. Chilean archaeologist Claudio Cristino and more than five hundred workers start restoring the ahu at Tongariki. This large ahu is in bad shape. Ancient events probably damaged it. In addition, a tsunami (huge sea wave) hit the island in 1960. The wave knocked the ahu's moai, pukao, and blocks far inland. Statues and debris cover an area of 5 acres (2 hectares).

A Japanese company donates a giant crane and two million dollars to this project. Before the team moves the statues, they use chemicals to harden and protect the rock. They also repair one statue that has lost its 27-ton (24-metric-ton) head. They carefully replace the head using more than 80 tons (73 metric tons) of a special kind of cement. By 1997 moai once again stand proudly at Tongariki.

HOW TO MOVE A MOAI

After all these years, the same big secret still remains. How did Easter Islanders

The restored ahu and moai at Tongariki stand behind a statue that still lies on the ground.

Jo Anne Van Tilburg (right) and a member of her team put a grid on a moai statue on Easter Island in 1991. They are measuring the statue to make a computer image of it for further study.

move the moai into place? In April 1998, a group of experts comes to investigate the puzzle. Jo Anne Van Tilburg leads the international group, which includes archaeologists Claudio Cristino and Edmundo Edwards. The team also includes architects, construction experts, an artist, and an engineer. They plan to do an experiment that they think could put the long debate to rest.

Using an ancient statue for the experiment is far too risky. So the team's first step is to make its own moai. But hand carving one would take too long. Instead, engineers in the United States make a hollow mold out of a light material called fiberglass. They send it to the team on Easter Island. Team members fill the finished mold with a mixture of concrete and red scoria. In the end, the team has a 13-foot-tall (4 m), 12-ton (11-metric-ton) statue. It is similar in size and weight to an average moai.

The experts think that islanders moved moai on wooden sleds called sledges. Ancient Polynesians once used sledges to move giant canoes. Workers pulled these sledges across logrollers lying on the ground.

The team has seen signs of ancient roads on the island. They think these roads were once transport routes for statues from Rano Raraku to all parts of the island. But did past islanders use sledges for the job? Research shows that palm trees thrived on the island before A.D. 1600. These trees could have provided trunks for rollers and sleds.

Palm trees are no longer common on the island. But large eucalyptus trees are available. To test their theory, the team directs workers to build a V-shaped sledge out of eucalyptus trees. Meanwhile, another crew builds a replica of an ahu. A 130-foot (40 m) earthen ramp leads up to the flat platform. The team's goal is to raise the moai onto the ahu.

A SLIPPERY SOLUTION

The team lays down a 120-foot-long (37 m) track made of eucalyptus logs. They place free-rolling logs on top of the track. Then they use a modern crane to place their statue faceup on the sledge. The team has attached ropes to the sledge.

The team decides that forty people will pull. Six others will keep the rollers in line. After counting to three in the Rapanui language, the group pulls together. The sledge moves easily on the slippery rollers. But suddenly the logs slip off the track. The experiment grinds to a halt. The team tries again, but the same thing happens.

Van Tilburg thinks they should tie some of the rollers to the sledge. She has seen this technique used in canoe ladders. Ancient Polynesians used these framelike structures to move 5- to 10-ton (4.5- to 9-metric-ton) wooden boats. Although the logs will no longer be able to roll, they should still slide across the tracks. Once again, the pullers give the ropes a mighty tug. This time the sledge flies along the tracks. With two pulls, the sledge moves about 360 feet (110 m). Team members and volunteers celebrate wildly.

Jo Anne Van Tilburg and her team lower the replica statue faceup onto the logs. They are testing one theory of how ancient islanders moved moai.

The team does one more experiment. They try moving the moai up a small hill. They do not use rollers. Instead, they use a method based on Polynesian boat ladders. They place logs at several points across the tracks. Team members have greased the logs and the bottom of the sledge with a liquid from the stumps of banana trees. The team pulls on the ropes one more time. The slippery liquid helps it slide easily along the tracks—even uphill.

Soon the team has pulled the sledge and its moai all the way to the front of the ahu ramp. Another strong tug slides it up the slope and onto the platform. With one more day of positioning, the team lines up the statue's base with the ahu.

Finally, it is time to place the moai upright on the ahu. Using logs as levers, workers tip the statue upward from the sledge. They move it only a few inches at a time. Meanwhile, they slip supporting logs underneath. The moai rises steadily. With one final pull on ropes tied around it, the moai settles onto its platform. The experiment is a success! The experiment proves that early islanders could have moved a moai across flat ground and up slopes using a sledge and a track.

DEFENDING EACH THEORY

Not everyone is convinced the ancient Rapanui actually used this method, however. For example, some experts don't think it would have worked in cramped parts of the island.

Eventually, the team agrees that ancient people probably used a variety of methods to move the massive rocks. Different situations needed different approaches. Most important, the experiment shows that a fairly small group of people could have moved and erected a moai. Members of one family could have put up their own statues.

Meanwhile, EISP project investigators continue gathering information about the moai. Their work goes on into the 2000s. The EISP files hold twelve thousand picture records. They cover 887 moai at 210 sites, out of an estimated 313 total moai locations on the island. Their survey also includes information about 55 Easter Island statues in museums around the world. The project remains the largest and longest archaeological study of Easter Island ever conducted.

Sunset falls over the statues at Ahu Tahai on Easter Island. The island has become a popular destination for tourists.

EPILOGUE

New generations of scientists and researchers kept on studying Easter Island. Each group reexamined existing information and eagerly dug for more.

Over the years, new studies tended to contradict Thor Heyerdahl's ideas about Easter Island's first settlers. He had said they were master stoneworkers and sailors from Peru. But later studies of living Easter Islanders found no trace of South American genetic material. These findings seem to disprove Heyerdahl's theory.

Even the often-repeated story about great tribal battles on the island has fallen by the wayside. Researchers have never found any clear evidence of ancient wars. For example, excavation has not revealed the large numbers of human remains that war would have left behind. And while visitors have found many obsidian spearpoints called *mata'a*, some

This obsidian spearpoint, called mata'a, was found on Easter Island.

archaeologists think that they may not have been weapons. Instead, mata'a could have been agricultural tools. Maybe localized or islandwide war never really took place.

Another type of competition may have affected Easter Island's fate, however. The most common idea of the past decade describes a terrible environmental collapse. At some point, some experts say, statue building became very competitive. Various family groups struggled to create the best moai. This competition may have grown so fierce that it damaged the island's fragile environment. Conditions finally reached a tipping point when workers cut down the last large tree. By destroying their island's trees, the people brought environmental disaster on themselves. Most of their food sources—animals, fish, birds, and plants—were used up or disappeared. Social chaos followed. Desperate and starving people revolted. They overthrew their rulers—along with the stone symbols of their oppression.

But another recent theory suggests that perhaps the Easter Islanders were not careless—just unlucky. Some researchers believe that rats might have invaded the island and wiped out the island's bird and plant food resources around A.D. 1200. Other experts blame unusual weather conditions in ancient times. Long dry spells might have led to loss of trees and food crops.

Not all scientists agree on any one theory about Easter Island's fate. But most do believe that an explosion in stone carving and statue building took place during hard times on the island. Putting up more monuments may have been the Rapanui's way of asking powerful ancestors for help. But the extra effort took extra resources. More and more food went to feed workers and carvers. Maybe the moai themselves doomed the island.

Whatever happened, Rapa Nui's people still accomplished great things. How many other cultures have ever made so much from so little?

Research and digs at Easter Island continue to reveal more and more facts. Experts continue to argue and learn. One thing they all agree on is that the puzzle of Easter Island's past is far more difficult than it once appeared. Every new idea is really an educated guess. And each theory requires testing and rethinking whenever new information comes to light. That is what archaeology is all about—constantly seeking new clues to gain a better understanding of the past.

Save the Moai!

Every year more and more visitors flock to Easter Island. They are eager to experience its mystery and beauty. Many hotels, restaurants, and shops have sprung up. But all this development on such a tiny island can be harmful. In fact, human impact has already damaged or destroyed many of Easter Island's moai and archaeological sites. To better study or view the statues, well-meaning people—even scientists—have harmed the statues by digging them out and standing them up again. Some people feel it may be wiser to leave them in their buried, fallen state. Easter Islanders face many difficult decisions about how to protect their ancient heritage.

These moai are just some of the statues that have been restored on Easter Island.

MAJOR MOAI OF EASTER ISLAND

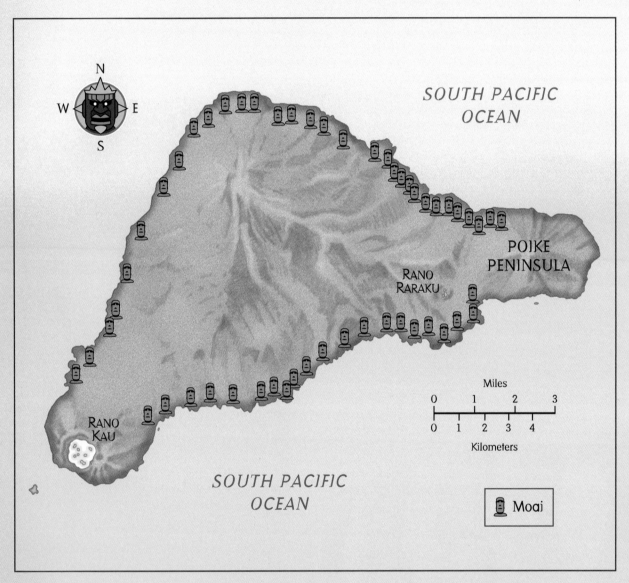

This map shows just a few of Easter Island's many moai. Altogether, more than 800 of the statues are on the island. As the map shows, Easter Islanders placed most of their statues along the island's coast. Over the centuries, the sight of these impressive moai has greeted sailors and other visitors to the island.

TIMELINE

Few archaeologists agree on early dates of events on Easter Island. For example, scientists have estimated the earliest settlement dates to be anywhere from A.D. 200–400 to 1400–1600. In the timeline below, the dates before 1722 are educated guesses that some scientists accept and others reject.

CA. 400
The first settlers arrive on Easter Island (Rapa Nui).

700–1000
Islanders, calling themselves Rapanui, build ceremonial complexes and moai.

1200s
Moai building increases. Shortages of food and natural resources become a problem.

1400s
Most of the island's trees are gone. Statue building is at a peak.

1500s
Warfare sweeps on Easter Island. Statue building at Rano Raraku ends, as the birdman cult develops.

1700s
The birdman cult slowly begins to decline.

1722
Dutch explorers led by Jacob Roggeveen visit the island. Roggeveen gives it the name Easter Island.

1770
Don Felipe Gonzalez de Haedo and his crew visit and claim the island for Spain.

1774
British explorer James Cook visits the island.

1862
Peruvian slave traders kidnap two thousand Rapanui.

1865
Returning islanders and visitors bring the deadly disease smallpox to Easter Island.

1868
The British ship *Topaze* visits, and its crew takes Hoa Hakananai'a to Great Britain.

1886
Crew members of the U.S. ship *Mohican* explore the island. Paymaster William Thomson leads the group.

1888
Chile takes control of Easter Island.

1914
Katherine and Scoresby Routledge arrive on the *Mana*.

1935
Chile establishes Rapa Nui National Park, covering all of Easter Island.

1952
Thor Heyerdahl's movie *Kon-Tiki* wins an Academy Award.

1955
Thor Heyerdahl arrives with his team of experts.

1960
A tsunami strikes the island and damages the ahu at Tongariki.

1965
Easter Island becomes a province of Chile.

1968
William Mulloy returns to Easter Island. Soon he and fellow experts begin a major project recording each statue and monument on the island.

1992
Chilean archaeologist Claudio Cristino and his team restore Tongariki's ahu.

1996
Rapa Nui National Park becomes a United Nations Educational, Scientific, and Cultural Organization (UNESCO) World Heritage Site.

1998
A group of experts carry out an experiment in moving a moai.

2002
Thor Heyerdahl dies.

2007
A new luxury hotel opens on Easter Island in December.

PRONUNCIATION GUIDE

Below is a pronunciation key to some of the names and terms used in this book. Notice the upside-down apostrophe in *Hotu Matu'a* and several other words and phrases. In the Rapanui language, this symbol shows a break before an ending vowel, like the one in the middle of the phrase *uh-oh*.

ahu	AH-hoo
Anakena	ah-nuh-KAY-nuh
Hoa Hakananai'a	HOH-uh HAH-kah-NAH-nah-EE-uh
Hotu Matu'a	HOE-too mah-too-EH
Make-Make	MAH-kay MAH-kay
mana	MAH-nuh
mata'a	mah-tah-EH
moai	moh-EYE
Motu Nui	MOH-too NOO-ee
Orongo	oh-RONG-goh
Poike	poy-KEH
poki-manu	POE-kee MAH-noo
pukao	poo-KOW
Rano Kau	RAHN-oh KOW
Rano Raraku	RAHN-oh ruh-RAH-koo
Rapa Nui	RAH-puh NOO-ee
rongo-rongo	RONG-oh-RONG-oh
toki	TOH-kee
Tongariki	tahn-gah-REE-kee
Vinapu	VEEN-ah-poo

GLOSSARY

ahu: a ceremonial stone platform, often used as a burial site. Some of Easter Island's moai once sat on ahu. Many ahu were part of larger ceremonial complexes.

aringa ora: a traditional name for the island's statues. The words literally mean "living faces."

artifact: objects or the remains of objects made by people who lived in the past

Hotu Matu'a: the traditional chief, or king, who, legend says, led the first colonists to Easter Island. The name means "Great Parent."

Make-Make: the name of the great "Creator Spirit" in Easter Island tradition and culture

mana: spiritual power or influence

mata'a: an obsidian spearpoint. Archaeologists once thought the mata'a were weapons. But later researchers have suggested they may have been for farming, not fighting.

moai: the stone statues of Easter Island. Most experts think the moai represent former kings or wise men. The word comes from the Polynesian word for "wise one" or "ancient ancestor."

Orongo: a currently deserted ceremonial village on Rano Kau on Easter Island's southern coast. Orongo was the center of bird cult religious rituals until the late 1800s, when islanders seem to have abandoned both the cult and the village.

poki-manu: children who took part in rituals related to the bird cult. The name literally means "bird children."

pukao: a crownlike hat, or headdress, placed on the heads of some of the moai that sat on ahu. Pukao are made of the volcanic stone red tufa. Islanders apparently added pukao to some moai as a sign of honor.

Rapa Nui: a Polynesian name for Easter Island. Most modern islanders use this name. The people of the island and the language they speak are called Rapanui.

rongo-rongo: an ancient written form of the Rapanui language. Researchers have found rongo-rongo symbols carved on ancient wooden tablets on Easter Island. These tablets are also called rongo-rongo. Sometimes they are also called "talking boards." They may tell the history or stories of Easter Island's people and origins. But none of these boards have been translated.

toki: traditional wedge-shaped stone tools made of basalt or obsidian. Easter Islanders used toki to carve moai and pukao.

WHO'S WHO?

Thor Heyerdahl (1914–2002) Born in Larvik, Norway, Thor Heyerdahl always had a taste for adventure. After graduation from the University of Oslo in 1936, he and his wife sailed to the Polynesian islands. In Polynesia, Heyerdahl developed a fascination for Pacific history. He also developed his theory about Easter Island's South American ancestors. After his 1947 *Kon-Tiki* adventure and his 1955 Easter Island expedition, Heyerdahl made three long-distance trips in reed ships modeled on ancient sailing boats. The first two voyages crossed the Atlantic Ocean in papyrus ships called *Ra I* and *Ra II.* These trips were attempts to prove that ancient boats could have survived ocean voyages. In the 1980s and 1990s, Heyerdahl went to Peru to study ancient pyramids. He wrote many books about his experiences. They included *Kon-Tiki* (1950), *Aku-Aku: The Secret of Easter Island* (1958), and *The Art of Easter Island* (1975). Thor Heyerdahl later dedicated much of his time to antiwar and humanitarian projects. He died at the age of eighty-seven.

Katherine Pease Routledge (1866–1935) Katherine Routledge was born in Darlington, England, into a wealthy Quaker family. She was one of the first women to attend classes at Oxford University, where she studied anthropology and history. She married the British anthropologist William Scoresby Routledge in 1906. In 1910 the Routledges published a book called *With a Prehistoric People.* The book discussed the Kikuyu people of eastern Africa. It was so successful that the British Museum asked the Routledges to go to Easter Island and document its archaeology and oral traditions. Their trip became the first official scientific investigation of the island. They arrived in March 1914 and spent nearly a year and a half there. They surveyed archaeological sites and recorded stories told by islanders. In 1919 she published a book *The Mystery of Easter Island.* But illness prevented her from returning to the island, and she never finished writing the full scientific report that she had planned. By the time she died, most of her field notes and expedition records had become scattered and largely forgotten. Many of her papers were later rediscovered. Her skillful research and writing reveal important insights about Easter Island.

William Judah Thomson (1841–1909) Born in Washington, D.C., William Thomson joined the U.S. Navy in 1865, right after the Civil War (1861–1865). In 1886 the U.S. Navy sent the USS *Mohican* to Easter Island. The crew had instructions to explore the island and collect whatever plant and archaeological specimens and information it could find and send them to the National Museum in Washington, D.C. Thomson was the ship's paymaster (the officer responsible for pay, food, clothing, and other items sailors might need while aboard). He was delighted when he was placed in charge of the expedition. Although he was not a trained scientist, he had helped in the excavation of several sites in Peru. He was also a careful observer. The *Mohican*'s eleven-day stay at Easter Island resulted in a rich report that contained much more than plant and animal data. Thomson's report remains one of the most detailed and accurate early sources of information about Easter Island's archaeology and culture.

Jo Anne Van Tilburg (b. 1940s) Born in Minneapolis, Minnesota, Jo Anne Van Tilburg is an experienced archaeologist. She is one of the world's leading authorities on Easter Island's moai. She is also a specialist in Polynesian studies. Van Tilburg has done a great deal of fieldwork on Easter Island, as well as in the Micronesian Republic of Palau. As director of the Easter Island Statue Project, Van Tilburg has worked for more than twenty years to discover, describe, and conserve Easter Island's moai.

SOURCE NOTES

8 Bolton Glanville Corney, *The Voyage of Captain Don Felipe Gonzalez in the Ship of the Line San Lorenzo with the Frigate Santa Rosalia in Company to Easter Island in 1770–1: Preceded by an Extract from Mynheer Jacob Roggeveen's Official Log of His Discovery of and Visit to Easter Island in 1722* (Cambridge, UK: Hakluyt Society, 1908), 15.

8 Ibid., 16.

8 Ibid., 15.

10 James Cook, *Second Voyage towards the South Pole and Round the World, Performed in the Resolution and Adventure, 1722–75*, 2 vols. (London: W. Strahan and T. Cadell, 1777), 281.

10 Ibid.

10–11 Ibid., 288.

19 William Judah Thomson, *Te Pito Henua, or Easter Island, Report of the U.S. National Museum for the Year Ending June 30, 1889* (Washington, DC: U.S. Government Printing Office, 1889), 498.

28 Ibid., 493.

30 Ibid., 512.

34 Katherine Routledge, *The Mystery of Easter Island* (London: Sifton, Praed and Company), 1919), 171.

38 Ibid., 264.

47 William Mulloy, "The Ceremonial Center of Vinapu," in Thor Heyerdahl and Edwin N. Ferdon, eds., *The Archaeology of Easter Island: Reports of the Norwegian Archaeological Expedition to Easter Island and the East Pacific*, vol. 1 (London: Allen and Unwin, 1961), 100.

55 Thor Heyerdahl, *Aku-Aku: The Secret of Easter Island* (New York: Rand McNally, 1958), 87.

SELECTED BIBLIOGRAPHY

Cook, James. *Second Voyage towards the South Pole and Round the World, Performed in the Resolution and Adventure, 1722–75.* 2 vols. London: W. Strahan and T. Cadell, 1777.

Corney, Bolton Glanville. *The Voyage of Captain Don Felipe Gonzalez in the Ship of the Line San Lorenzo with the Frigate Santa Rosalia in Company to Easter Island in 1770–1: Preceded by an Extract from Mynheer Jacob Roggeveen's Official Log of His Discovery of and Visit to Easter Island in 1722.* Cambridge, UK: Hakluyt Society, 1908.

Ferdon, Edwin. *One Man's Log.* New York: Rand McNally, 1966.

Heyerdahl, Thor. *Aku-Aku: The Secret of Easter Island.* New York: Rand McNally, 1958.

Mulloy, William. "The Ceremonial Center of Vinapu." In Thor Heyerdahl and Edwin N. Ferdon, eds. *The Archaeology of Easter Island and the East Pacific.* Vol. 1. London: Allen and Unwin, 1961.

Lavachery, Henri. "Easter Island, Polynesia." *Antiquity,* March 1938, 53–60.

Métraux, Alfred. "Mysteries of Easter Island." *PTO,* October 1939, 33–47.

Mulloy, William. *The Easter Island Bulletins of William Mulloy.* Houston: World Monument Fund and Easter Island Foundation, 1997.

Routledge, Katherine. *The Mystery of Easter Island.* London: Sifton, Praed and Company, 1919.

Thomson, William Judah. *Te Pito Henua, or Easter Island, Report of the U.S. National Museum for the Year Ending June 30, 1889.* Washington, DC: U.S. Government Printing Office, 1889, 447–552.

Van Tilburg, Jo Anne. *Easter Island Archaeology, Ecology and Culture.* London: British Museum Press, 1994.

———."First EISP Field Season." *Easter Island Statue Project.* N.d. http://ioa.ucla.edu/eisp/history/historyframe.htm (January 7, 2008).

FURTHER READING AND WEBSITES

BOOKS

Arnold, Caroline. *Easter Island: Giant Stone Statues Tell of a Rich and Tragic Past.* New York: Clarion Books, 2000.

Barron, T. A., and William Low. *The Day the Stones Walked.* New York: Philomel, 2007.

DiPiazza, Francesca Davis. *Chile in Pictures.* Minneapolis: Twenty-First Century Books, 2007.

Heyerdahl, Thor. *Kon-Tiki: Across the Pacific by Raft.* Chicago: Rand McNally, 1950.

McLaughlin, Shawn. *The Complete Guide to Easter Island.* Los Osos, AZ: Easter Island Foundation, 2004.

O'Neill, Katrina, and Brenda Cantrell. *Racing for the Birdman.* New York: Facts On File, 2005.

Orliac, Catherine, and Michel Orliac. *Easter Island: Mystery of the Stone Giants.* Translated by Paul G. Bahn. New York: Harry N. Abrams, 1995.

Pelta, Kathy. *Rediscovering Easter Island.* Minneapolis: Twenty-First Century Books, 2001.

Simmons, Alex. *Mysteries of the Past: A Chapter Book.* Danbury, CT: Children's Press, 2007.

Van Tilburg, Jo Anne. *Among Stone Giants: The Life of Katherine Routledge and Her Remarkable Voyage to Easter Island.* New York: Scribner's, 2003.

WEBSITES

Easter Island
http://www.mysteriousplaces.com/Easter_Island/index.html
Read about Easter Island's people, explore its history, and take a tour of the island—complete with pictures!

Mystic Places: Easter Island
http://exn.ca/mysticplaces/easterisland.asp
Visit this site from Discovery Channel for pictures, background information, and more.

Secrets of Lost Empires: Easter Island
http://www.pbs.org/wgbh/nova/lostempires/easter/
Explore Easter Island and its mysteries with this website from PBS's *NOVA* program.

INDEX

ABOUT THE AUTHOR

Michael Capek is the author of numerous stories, articles, and books for young readers, including *Emperor Qin's Terra Cotta Army*, *A Ticket to Jamaica*, and *A Personal Tour of Shaker Village*. He is a retired English teacher and a native Kentuckian. His interest in archaeological mysteries goes back to when he searched the fields and streams near his childhood home for arrowheads, wondering who left them and what their lives were like. He feels that same sense of wonder about the ancient people of Easter Island.

PHOTO ACKNOWLEDGMENTS

The images in this book are used with the permission of: © Cliff Wassmann, pp. 4, 16 (both), 24, 27, 29 (both), 42, 46, 48, 49, 63; Courtesy of the Easter Island Foundation, pp. 5, 12, 33, 34, 57; National Anthropological Archives, Smithsonian Institution: p. 6, NAA INV 47300; p. 13, NAA INV 04948603; p. 25, NAA INV 04949300; © Peter Miller/Alamy, p. 8; © Smithsonian American Art Museum, Washington D.C./Art Resource, NY, p. 11; © John Kreul/Independent Picture Service, pp. 14, 56, 65; © John Warburton-Lee/Danita Delimont/drr.net, p. 20; © George Holton/Photo Researchers, Inc., p. 22; © Shawn McLaughlin, pp. 17 (both), 26, 32, 58, 64; © National Geographic Society Image Collection, p. 35; Royal Geographical Society 2005, pp. 36, 39, 41; © Copyright The British Museum, gift of W. Scoresby Routledge, p. 37; © Hulton-Deutsch Collection/CORBIS, p. 43; © Christophe Boisvieux/CORBIS, p. 44; ; © Lee Foster/drr.net, p. 52 © Shawn McLaughlin with the kind permission of MAPSE, p. 54; © James L. Amos/Peter Arnold, Inc., p. 59; © 1998 EISP/JVT/Photo: J. Van Tilburg, p. 60. Illustrations by © Laura Westlund/Independent Picture Service.

Front cover: © Joseph Van Os/Stone/Getty Images.